ve written. It was started
in its final format with
lson. She has been a
I trust it will be a
the study of the

COLOSSIANS
THE THINGS ABOVE

DONALD NORBIE

CONTENTS

INTRODUCTION

It was on Paul's third missionary journey that he stayed in Ephesus for a lengthy period from 52-55 A.D. It was a strategic center for evangelizing the whole province of Asia. It was apparently during this time that Epaphras became a believer and later carried the gospel to Colossae. Paul himself apparently had never visited the city (Col. 1:4; 2:1). It was a smaller city in the beautiful Lycus valley. Laodicea and Hierapolis were larger cities in the area. Paul's stay in Ephesus was a very fruitful time.

Paul was later arrested in Jerusalem by Roman authorities who rescued him from a Jewish mob intent on killing him. From 57-59 A.D. Paul was imprisoned in Caesarea. Finally Paul appealed to Caesar for a resolution of his case. After an exciting voyage and shipwreck he arrived in Rome. As the book of Acts ends he is a house prisoner awaiting trial.

It was during this time from 60-62 A.D. that he wrote the wonderfully rich epistles of Ephesians, Philippians, Colossians and Philemon. They are the ripe fruit of a lifetime of studying God's Word and preaching the gospel. The Holy Spirit energized Paul in the expression of some of the deepest teaching of the Word of God.

The purpose of this letter was to correct some false teaching that was infiltrating the church. There was a strain of Jewish legalism with an emphasis on certain foods and the keeping of Jewish holidays. There were also certain Gnostic ideas which would become fully developed in the next century. Some of these teachings claimed to give one a deeper insight into truth, "philosophy." Matter was inherently evil and God was not the direct Creator. There were intermediate agencies.

Christ could not have actually taken on flesh since it is evil. Salvation came through human effort by gaining superior knowledge (*gnosis*), progressing upward to perfection. Since matter is evil and the human body is evil, part of salvation was an ascetic life style of self-denial. Paul urges them to get back to the reality of the greatness of the Person of Christ, His incarnation, and the adequacy of the gospel. Salvation was the work of Christ, not the result of human effort or superior knowledge.

The epistle to the Ephesians focuses on the church as the body of Christ. But Colossians emphasizes Christ as the Head of the church and of all of creation, that *"in all things he might have the preeminence"* (Col. 1:18).

The book divides nicely into two parts. Chapters 1 and 2 are doctrinal, confronting the doctrinal errors that were affecting them. Chapters 3 and 4 are practical. For Paul correct doctrine was not an end in itself, a matter of scholarly discussion. True doctrine should effect a radical change in the lives of believers.

"Let your light so shine before men, that they may see your good works, and glorify your Father which is in heaven" (Matt. 5:16).

Paul was released and spent several years in travel and teaching God's Word. During a wave of persecution Paul was arrested again. This time he was executed. As a Roman citizen he would have been beheaded and not crucified. And so ended the life of this great man of God. In his last letter to Timothy, his son in the faith, he wrote:

"For I am now ready to be offered, and the time of my departure is at hand. I have fought a good fight, I have finished my course, I have kept the faith: Henceforth there is laid up for me a crown of righteousness, which the Lord, the righteous judge, shall give me at that day: and not to me only, but unto all them also that love his appearing" (2 Tim. 4:6-8).

COLOSSIANS OUTLINE

Salutation (1:1-2)

Paul's Prayer (1:3-12)
- A. Thanksgiving for their Faith (1:3-8)
- B. Petition for their Growth (1:9-12)

Christ's Preeminence Part One (1:13-23)
- A. The Saviour of Mankind (1:13-14)
- B. The Image of God (1:15)
- C. The Creator and Sustainer of the Universe, Including Angels (1:16-17)

Christ's Preeminence Part Two (1:18-23)
- A. Head of the Church; Preeminent in Every Area (1:18)
- B. God's Fullness Dwells in Him (1:19)
- C. He Reconciled All Things to God Through the Cross (1:20-23)

Paul's Shepherd Care for the Church (1:24-2:5)
- A. Paul Brought them the Mystery of the Gospel, Christ (1:24-29)
  1. Paul's Ministry of Suffering
  2. Paul's Ministry of Stewardship
  3. Paul's Ministry of Salvation
  4. Paul's Ministry of Sanctification
- B. Paul's Struggle to See them Grow in their Knowledge of Christ (2:1-5)

Warning Against Legalism (2:6-23)
- A. Continue in Your Life in Christ (2:6-7)
- B. Beware of False Teachers (2:8)
- C. Christ is the Fullness of Deity and Authority (2:9-10)
- D. Spiritual Circumcision of the Flesh, New Life (2:11-12)
- E. The Law Against Us Cancelled (2:13-14)
- F. Evil Angelic Forces Defeated by the Cross (2:15)
- G. Reject Jewish Legalism, Festivals and Mysticism (2:16-19)
- H. You Died with Christ; Do Not Go Back to Food Laws or Asceticism (2:20-23)

Holy Living Part One (3:1-17)
  A. Motivation: Focus on Christ and Heaven (3:1-4)
  B. Put to Death Your Sinful Nature: Sexual Sins, Evil Desires, Greed, Rage, Slander, Filthy Talk, Lying (3:5-9a)

Holy Living Part Two (3:9b-17)
  A. You Have Put on the New Man, Which Needs Daily Renewal (3:9b-11)
  B. Clothe Yourself Daily with: Compassion, Kindness, Humility, Gentleness, Patience, Forgiveness and Love Over All (3:12-14)
  C. Aids to Godliness: A Heart at Peace Filled with God's Word, Sharing the Word and Singing, Doing All in Christ's Name (3:15-17)

Holy Families (3:18-4:6)
  A. Wives to Submit to Husbands (3:18)
  B. Husbands to Love Wives (3:19)
  C. Children to Obey Parents; Fathers to be Gentle (3:20-21)
  D. Slaves, Servants, be Obedient; Work for the Lord (3:22-25)
  E. Masters, be Fair and Kind (4:1)
  F. Further Advice (4:2-6)
      1. Pray Much, Especially for Paul. (4:2-4)
      2. Be Wise in Your Witnessing. (4:5-6)

Concluding Greetings (4:7-18)
  A. Tychicus and Onesimus will Give the News About Me (4:7-9)
  B. Aristarchus, a Fellow Prisoner, Mark, Justus, Who are Jews, Send Greetings (4:10-11)
  C. Epaphras, One of You, Prays Much for You, Laodiceas and Hierapolis. (4:12-13)
  D. Dr. Luke and Demas Send Greetings (4:14)
  E. Greet Brothers in Laodicea and the Church in Nympha's House (4:15)
  F. Share Letters with Laodicea (4:16)

COLOSSIANS OUTLINE

G. Archipus, Finish Your Work (4:17)
H. Remember My Chains. Grace be With You. Hand
    Written, Paul (4:18)

CHAPTER 1

SALUTATION

Colossians 1:1-2

Paul, an apostle of Jesus Christ by the will of God, and Timotheus our brother, To the saints and faithful brethren in Christ which are at Colosse: Grace be unto you, and peace, from God our Father and the Lord Jesus Christ.   Colossians 1:1-2

Paul begins his letter to the church at Colosse with his own name. He has never been there but regards them as his spiritual children. While he was in Ephesus for about three years he obtained the use of the school of Tyrannus and taught there daily (Acts 19:9-10). God worked in a powerful way through Paul's teaching and miracles that he performed. The gospel spread through the whole Roman province of Asia. Epaphras and others who were converted were zealous in spreading the message. Now Epaphras has come to visit Paul in Rome, where he is awaiting trial as one comes to the end of the book of Acts. He brings news of the blessing in Colosse but also concern over certain false teaching that is creeping into the church.

Paul reminds them of the authority he has as an apostle. Paul is aware that he is inspired of God and speaks with the authority of God (1 Cor. 14:37). Now Paul is about to exercise his authority by defining what their teaching and practice should be. Like the prophets of old he is very conscious that God has called him to this ministry. Amos could say when threatened and warned to stop preaching,

I was no prophet, neither was I a prophet's son; but I was an herdman, and a gatherer of sycomore fruit: And the Lord took me as I followed the flock, and the Lord said unto me, Go, prophesy unto my people Israel.   Amos 7:14-15

This call of God makes the servant of God fearless.

Paul includes Timothy in the greeting, calling him *"our brother."* Timothy was very dear to Paul, being his son in the faith, having been led to Christ by Paul on his first missionary journey. On his second journey with Silas they chose Timothy to accompany them (Acts 16:1-3). Timothy was faithful and well spoken of by the disciples in the area. This began a long fruitful relationship with Paul that lasted until Paul's death. Paul's last letter was to Timothy before his execution in Rome.

Paul addresses the believers as *"saints and faithful brethren."* Saints (*hagioi*, Gk.) were those who were consecrated to a god to serve him. When sinners are converted and become believers in the Lord Jesus they are at that moment consecrated as priests and should live holy lives. Peter states that we are a *"holy priesthood"* (1 Pet. 2:5).

They are *"faithful brethren,"* members of God's wonderful family. One does not join a family; he is born into it, sharing the same life inherited from the Father. They are faithful, strong in their faith in the true and living God, not seduced by the idolatry and immorality which surrounded them.

"Grace...and peace" the Greek and Hebrew greetings are combined as are the Jew and Gentile in the church. Grace precedes peace in the heart of the believer. *"Therefore being justified by faith, we have peace with God through our Lord Jesus Christ"* (Rom. 5:1). Justification takes place at the moment of conversion; it is not something we obtain after a life of godly living. It is based on Christ's death for us not on our life for God. God's law is satisfied (Gal. 3:13) and we have peace with God. The enmity is over (Rom. 5:10).

Paul speaks of God as *"our Father;"* we are members of God's family. The Prodigal was received back into the family. And Christ is addressed as Deity on the same level as the Father, *"the Lord Jesus Christ."* Paul affirms from the start of his letter the exalted, unique position of Jesus. There was a time when he was rabid in his hatred of Christ and His followers. Now he speaks reverently of Him as Lord. Thank God!

CHAPTER 2

PAUL'S PRAYER

Colossians 1:3-12

A. Thanksgiving for their Faith (1:3-8)

We give thanks to God and the Father of our Lord Jesus Christ, praying always for you, Since we heard of your faith in Christ Jesus, and of the love which ye have to all the saints. Colossians 1:3-4

Paul often in his letters begins with a commendation of his readers. He is thankful for their salvation and spiritual growth. He has heard of their faith, not having visited them personally. But they are his spiritual grandchildren and have a special place in his prayers. Follow his example and look for the good in other believers. This will temper your criticism of them. And remember, they are saints, God's sanctified priesthood, a holy people. Believers need to be reminded of this often and live holy lives, remembering their calling.

For the hope which is laid up for you in heaven, whereof ye heard before in the word of the truth of the gospel; Which is come unto you, as it is in all the world; and bringeth forth fruit, as it doth also in you, since the day ye heard of it, and knew the grace of God in truth: As ye also learned of Epaphras our dear fellowservant, who is for you a faithful minister of Christ; Who also declared unto us your love in the Spirit. Colossians 1:5-8

This world culture is permeated with lies, utterly deceived by the father of lies, the devil (John 8:44). The gospel shines a beam of truth into the heart proclaiming the truth of the need for repentance toward God and faith in the Lord Jesus Christ.

To the sinner who repents and receives Christ the promise of hope in heaven is given. Peter speaks of *"an inheritance incorruptible, and undefiled, and that fadeth not away, reserved in heaven for you"* (1 Pet. 1:4). The stock market and banks may fail. Property values may plunge. But the believer's retirement is secure in the vaults of heaven. In view of this the exhortation of Jesus is to invest in that secure place.

> *Lay not up for yourselves treasures upon earth, where moth and rust doth corrupt, and where thieves break through and steal: But lay up for yourselves treasures in heaven, where neither moth nor rust doth corrupt, and where thieves do not break through nor steal: For where your treasure is, there will your heart be also.*   Matthew 6:19-21

Paul speaks of the *"truth of the gospel"* (v. 5). Those early apostles and evangelists were convinced that their message was true. They were convinced of the historic reality of the death, burial and resurrection of Christ. He is the Messiah, the longing hope of Israel. Peter could speak of them as *"eyewitnesses"* (2 Pet. 1:16). Men will not die for a lie if they know it is a lie. These men sealed their testimony with their blood.

Paul describes the gospel as having spread throughout the cosmos (*kosmos*, Gk.), the world of Roman culture around the Mediterranean Sea. This was the world that Paul knew. The message had been fruitful, leading people to Jesus Christ and changing lives morally. This was because evangelism was not left to the apostles. All of the believers were excited about the message and were fervent in spreading the word. As persecution spread after Stephen's death, *"they that were scattered abroad went every where preaching the word"* (Acts 8:4). The message had come to them and was bearing fruit among them. It was a message of the grace of God, not a religion of rituals and rules to gain favor with God.

It was Epaphras who had brought this glorious message to them. Paul describes him as a *"dear fellowservant,"* (v.

7) literally "fellowslave" (*sundoulos*, Gk.). Paul never pulled rank on younger men. He is also described as *"faithful"* (v. 7), one Paul could trust. And he was a *"minister of Christ"* (v. 7) (*diakonos*, Gk.), emphasizing his activity among them as Christ's servant, not a clergyman. In their relationship to God they were slaves. Epaphras had brought Paul a glowing report of their love in the Spirit. Love is the fruit of the Spirit and evidence of new life within them. This caused Paul to be thankful and to rejoice.

B. Petition for their Growth (1:9-12)

For this cause we also, since the day we heard it, do not cease to pray for you, and to desire that ye might be filled with the knowledge of his will in all wisdom and spiritual understanding; That ye might walk worthy of the Lord unto all pleasing, being fruitful in every good work, and increasing in the knowledge of God; Strengthened with all might, according to his glorious power, unto all patience and longsuffering with joyfulness; Giving thanks unto the Father, which hath made us meet to be partakers of the inheritance of the saints in light

Colossians 1:9-12

Because Epaphras has brought news of the spiritual condition there, Paul has been moved to pray fervently for them and now to write this letter. There is so much error and confusion in the world generated by the father of lies, the devil (John 8:44). False religions arise professing to have a deeper insight into spiritual truth, adding to the Scriptures their own writings and books. Satan can confuse and seduce believers away from the truth and render them useless to God.

The remedy for error is the truth proclaimed vigorously and fearlessly. Paul prays that they may be filled with the knowledge (*epignosis*, Gk., knowledge intensified) of God's will and get true spiritual understanding. The Gnostics and other such movements prided themselves on having deeper knowledge, (*gnosis*, Gk.) of spiritual truth. The antidote of error is not just to empty the mind of error but to fill it with truth. The Lord told the parable of a demon leaving a house. Later he came back, found the house empty and recruited seven other demons and they occupied the house. The man's last condition was worse than before. Paul exhorts them not to just empty their thinking of evil but to fill it with the truth. Fill your minds with knowledge of God's will so you make wise, understanding choices. And where will we get such wisdom so that our thinking is right and we make wise decisions?

Psalm one describes such a godly man.

> *Blessed is the man that walketh not in the counsel of the ungodly, nor standeth in the way of sinners, nor sitteth in the seat of the scornful. But his delight is in the law of the* Lord; *and in his law doth he meditate day and night.* Psalm 1:1-2

The knowledge of God and His will certainly will make one wise. The Torah (instruction), God's Word, will keep him from error and enable him to make wise decisions in life. This is the man who will know true prosperity. And he will be walking, living a life that delights the heart of the Father. Should not the heart of the believer desire to please the Father who has qualified him (*hikano*, Gk., "to make sufficient or adequate") for heaven itself? If the Judge of all the earth qualifies one for heaven, nothing more need be done. To seek to add our works to what God has done in justifying us is to belittle Christ's death on the cross. His death is adequate to atone for the sins of all of mankind (1 John 2:1). The death of an infinite Person has infinite value.

This inheritance for us is kept secure in the vaults of heaven. This is *"an inheritance incorruptible, and undefiled, and that fadeth not away, reserved in heaven for you, Who are kept by the power of God through faith unto salvation ready to be revealed in the last time"* (1 Pet. 1:4-5). The believer then should be confident and happy, secure in the loving care of the Father. He has qualified all believers for heaven.

> I hear the words of love,
> I gaze upon the blood;
> I see the mighty sacrifice,
> And I have peace with God

Horatius Bonar
December 19, 1808 – May 31, 1889

CHAPTER 3

CHRIST'S PREEMINENCE *PART ONE*

Colossians 1:13-23

A. The Saviour of Mankind (1:13-14)

Who hath delivered us from the power of darkness, and hath translated us into the kingdom of his dear Son: In whom we have redemption through his blood, even the forgiveness of sins.   Colossians 1:13-14

Paul now moves from a focus on the believer and his salvation to center upon Christ and the greatness of His person and work. Christianity is not just a philosophy seeking to find meaning and purpose in life. And it is more than an ethical system with elaborate rules and regulations. It is a message about God becoming man to redeem His creatures. It is anchored in historical reality. Paul emphasizes this as he marshals a host of witnesses to verify Christ's rising from the dead (1 Cor. 15:5-8).

The Father has qualified us for heaven because of the work of the Son. It is because of the shedding of His blood, the giving of His life, that we can know redemption from the power and bondage of Satan. Like Israel in Egypt all of mankind was in slavery to sin and the devil. It was a bondage from which we could not extricate ourselves, but Christ, like Moses, has led us out of bondage.

Moses led them from the bondage of Egypt into a covenant relationship with God (Ex. 19-20). God was now their king. Believers are now in a covenant relationship with God, part of His kingdom and subject to His laws. Satan's kingdom is marked by spiritual and moral darkness, but now we are in the kingdom of light. Christian are now citizens of heaven, awaiting Christ's return (Phil. 3:20-21). They pray, *"Thy kingdom come"* (Matt. 6:10).

B. The Image of God (1:15)

Paul now moves into this magnificent description of the greatness of the person of the Christ, the Messiah. This high concept of the person of Christ did not evolve over the centuries but was fervently believed by Christians from the beginning.

> *He is the image of the invisible God, the firstborn*
> *over all creation.*   Colossians 1:15

Paul begins by emphasizing that Jesus is truly God. He is identical with the Father. They are two separate persons. When Jesus was here on earth He could pray to the Father and have fellowship with Him. As Son, He was submissive to the Father in rank. But He was identical with the Father in His essence. He is the image, the (*eikon*, Gk.), the exact image of the Father. He could say to those longing to see God, *"he that hath seen me hath seen the Father"* (John 14:9). The characteristics of Father and Son are identical. And He is *"the firstborn of every creature"* (Col. 1:15). This was a title given to the son and heir of the father. Ishmael was Abraham's first son, born to a slave. But Isaac was the "firstborn," Abraham's heir. So Israel is described as God's firstborn among the nations, His chosen people.

C. The Creator and Sustainer of the Universe, Including Angels (1:16-17)

> *For by him were all things created, that are in*
> *heaven, and that are in earth, visible and invisible,*
> *whether they be thrones, or dominions, or princi-*
> *palities, or powers: all things were created by him,*

*and for him: And he is before all things, and by him
all things consist*   Colossians 1:16-17

Paul now focuses on Christ's role as Creator. According to Genesis 1 the whole Trinity was involved: *"Let us make man in our image"* (Gen. 1:26). The One who became part of His creation was once the source of it all—the amazing mystery of the incarnation!

To Paul the spirit world of angels and demons that are ruled by Satan was very real. This evil domain was arranged in various units and ranks of authority. [There are also the good angels, loyal and serving God, *"ministering spirits"* (Heb. 1:14)]. At present this evil force dominates the world culture. Satan could claim the kingdoms of the world were his (Luke 4:6), a claim not disputed by our Lord. This evil kingdom will reign until Christ returns and set up His kingdom. Satan will be bound for a thousand years then released for a final rebellion. He and his demons are then cast into eternal hell (Rev. 20). But at present his rebellion is controlling this world and its culture.

Before the angel hosts were created and the universe spoken into existence, Jesus, the Messiah, was. He is timeless and eternal. He Himself made this claim to the incredulous Jews: *"Before Abraham was, I am"* (John 8:58). This claim His disciples believed then and still do today.

As the eternal God the Creator He also sustains the universe. By Him all things "consist" (*sunesteiken*, Gk., from sunisteimi, "to stand with or together"). All things are being held together in Christ. Paul could tell the Athenians of the greatness of his God. His God was not localized in some temple but filled the universe, *"For in him we live, and move, and have our being"* (Acts 17:28). Paul reveled in the greatness of his God, a Creator God, filling the whole universe. And this greatness he also attributes to Christ. He is the force that keeps this planet and all of the other heavenly bodies functioning and not disintegrating. Hebrews 1:3 describes Him as carrying (*phero*, Gk.) the universe along by the word of His power, a dynamic figure of speech. If one gets an understanding of the greatness of Christ, he will never be attracted by false religion or philosophy.

Crown Him with many crowns,
The Lamb upon His throne.
Hark! How the heav'nly anthem drowns
All music but its own.
Awake, my soul, and sing
Of Him who died for thee,
And hail Him as thy matchless king
Through all eternity.

Crown Him the Lord of years,
The potentate of time,
Creator of the rolling spheres,
Ineffably sublime.
All hail, Redeemer, hail!
For Thou has died for me;
Thy praise and glory shall not fail
Throughout eternity.

Matthew Bridges,
July 14, 1800 - October 6, 1894

CHAPTER 4

CHRIST'S PREEMINENCE *PART TWO*

Colossians 1:18-23

A. The Head of the Church: Preeminent in Every Area (1:18)

And he is the head of the body, the church: who is the beginning, the firstborn from the dead; that in all things he might have the preeminence.

Colossians 1:18

Who is the head of the church, the supreme authority? Christ is described as being the Head of the body, the church. Paul loves using the symbol of a human body for the church, emphasizing the spiritual unity of God's people and also the diversity of gifts among the members (Rom. 12; 1 Cor. 12). Christ is entitled to be the Head because He is the Creator and the Source of all life. But He is also entitled to such authority because He is uniquely the Redeemer. He has paid the redemption price by giving His life to pay for the sins of the whole world (1 John 2:1). No one else shares that unique glory (Rev. 5).

Although He calls the redeemed His brothers and sisters, He towers over them all. He is the Greatest. There are many tall peaks in Northern Colorado but one towers above them all, Longs Peak at 14,256 feet. It is preeminent, as is the Lord Jesus Christ.

He is also the *"beginning, the firstborn from the dead"* (Col. 1:18). Jesus was raised from the dead, the first of mankind to have a new, resurrection body. *"But now is Christ risen from the dead, and become the firstfruits of them that slept"* (1 Cor. 15:20). The first grain to ripen is a sample and a promise of the harvest to come. This too is His unique glory.

When one becomes a Christian he confesses that Jesus is Lord (Rom. 10:9). By doing this he acknowledges that Jesus is Deity and also that he is entering into a covenant relationship with Him. Every time one celebrates the Lord's Supper he confesses this binding relationship, a new covenant. The Lord Jesus is now his supreme authority. Too often salvation is proclaimed as a gift with no strings attached. Repentance is vital to salvation (Luke 13:3) and one should realize he is receiving the Giver as well as the gift. Christ is now his final authority.

As the head dominates and directs the body, Christ should direct and lead His church. The Bible is the guide book for the individual and for the local church (2 Tim. 3:14-16). Paul emphasizes that it is vital for a church to obey these instructions (1 Tim. 3:15). Today many churches disregard these commandments as irrelevant for this modern age. And yet in every age churches that have determined to obey these commands have known the blessing of God and the joy of obedience.

B. God's Fullness Dwells in Him (1:19)

For it pleased the Father that in him should all fulness dwell. Colossians 1:19

Various religions have claimed deity for their teachers or gurus. And some would claim that deity would come temporarily upon certain teachers. And so they give them worship as divine. The Japanese prior to the end of World War II claimed their emperor was divine and should be worshipped. Part of the peace agreement was that he must confess to his people that he was only a man. This was a tremendous blow to their faith.

But few of these heresies through the ages have claimed that the fullness of God was in a man. Jesus Christ claimed this for Himself. *"I and my Father are one"* (John 10:30). *"...he that hath seen me hath seen the Father"* (John 14:9). One must believe this is true. To become one of Jesus' disciples one must confess that He is Lord (Rom. 10:9). Confessing this truth, Christians have died for their faith through the ages. There is a great mystery here but His disciples then and still today believe this truth.

C. He Reconciled All Things to God
Through the Cross (1:20-23)

And, having made peace through the blood of his cross, by him to reconcile all things unto himself; by him, I say, whether they be things in earth, or things in heaven. And you, that were sometime alienated and enemies in your mind by wicked works, yet now hath he reconciled In the body of his flesh through death, to present you holy and unblameable and unreproveable in his sight: If ye continue in the faith grounded and settled, and be not moved away from the hope of the gospel, which ye have heard, and which was preached to every creature which is under heaven; whereof I Paul am made a minister.   Colossians 1:20-23

Paul now moves from the greatness of the person of Christ to His greatest work. As part of the Trinity He was a partner in the magnificent work of creating the universe. But now he moves on to consider the unique work that He alone could accomplish, the work of redemption.

Although the Father planned it and the Spirit predicted it through the prophets, Christ suffered, bled and died alone. There is a terrible loneliness in His cry, *"My God, my God, why hast thou forsaken me?"* (Matt. 27:46). His unique glory in John's heavenly vision is that He is the Lamb of God (Rev. 5). When He asked us to remember Him, He took bread and the cup, emblems of His cruel death for us. One can do nothing greater than to die for his fellow man. Christ is preeminent in His Deity, character, creative work and in His redemption of mankind.

When man sinned in Genesis 3, his act of rebellion affected mankind primarily but not alone. The earth also was cursed and is travailing as if in birth pains until now. *"For we know that the whole creation groaneth and travaileth in pain together until now"* (Rom. 8:22). When Christ returns and sets up His kingdom the birth pains will cease. And all of this is based on the redemptive work of Christ. This reconciliation reaches from earth to heaven. It is complete. Satan introduced a discordant note into the harmony of the universe. Christ by His death and atoning work brings harmony and peace. For it is by His death, the blood of the cross, that the ransom has been paid. The penalty of the broken Law of God is satisfied (Gal. 3:13). Christ's death has infinite value because of the infinite value of His Person as the Son of God. So the debt has been paid not only for believers but for the sins of the whole world (1 John 2:2). What an incentive to evangelize!

Paul now describes our relationship as believers to God. We *"were sometime alienated and enemies"* (v. 21), at war with God in both our minds and actions. Men like to speak of sins as mistakes. God describes sins as acts of rebellion, a defiance of the Almighty. Once we were enemies of God; now we are at peace with Him. Those who have fought in a war know the joy when hostilities have ceased and peace is proclaimed.

Now we stand before God *"holy and unblameable"* (v. 22). Believers are holy, spotless and pure. We stand blameless, no sins and failures of the past remembered. This is the saints' standing before God and this should give great joy and confidence in one's daily life.

But there is a word of caution lest one become complacent, *"If ye continue in the faith grounded and settled, and be not moved away from the hope of the gospel"* (v. 23). Saving faith is persevering and continuing. Do not rely on a past experience if there is no present reality. Too many have a false sense of security because of some past emotional, religious experience. Hell will be filled with people who thought they were going to heaven.

This glorious message of reconciliation is found in the gospel (1 Cor. 15:3-4). This message had spread through much of the Roman world, the known world of that day. Paul is very grateful that he has been called by God to this ministry, to proclaim the gospel. Ministry refers to service, not to the clergy. Although not having Paul's special call, all believers have the privilege of witnessing to the gospel and to its saving power. Do not be ashamed of your Lord.

> Jesus, and shall it ever be,
> A mortal man, ashamed of Thee?
> Ashamed of Thee, whom angels praise,
> Whose glories shine through endless days?
>
> Ashamed of Jesus! that dear friend
> On whom my hopes of Heav'n depend!
> No; when I blush, be this my shame,
> That I no more revere His name.

> Joseph Grigg,
> 1720-1768

CHAPTER 5

PAUL'S SHEPHERD CARE FOR THE CHURCH

Colossians 1:24-2:5

A. Paul Brought them the Mystery of the Gospel, Christ (1:24-29)

Who now rejoice in my sufferings for you, and fill up that which is behind of the afflictions of Christ in my flesh for his body's sake, which is the church: Whereof I am made a minister, according to the dispensation of God which is given to me for you, to fulfil the word of God; Even the mystery which hath been hid from ages and from generations, but now is made manifest to his saints: To whom God would make known what is the riches of the glory of this mystery among the Gentiles; which is Christ in you, the hope of glory: Whom we preach, warning every man, and teaching every man in all wisdom; that we may present every man perfect in Christ Jesus: Whereunto I also labour, striving according to his working, which worketh in me mightily.

Colossians 1:24-29

1. Paul's Ministry of Suffering

Paul talks of his ministry. First, it was a ministry of suffering. Usually we feel sorry for ourselves in suffering. Paul rejoices! He speaks of the joy he has suffering for Christ. He was in prison at the time. In Acts 5:40 Paul says, "*...when they had called*

31

the apostles, and beaten them, they commanded that they should not speak in the name of Jesus, and let them go". Here the apostles are threatened and beaten and they are told to quit preaching and talking about Jesus. As they leave, they are not feeling sorry for themselves but they are rejoicing that they were counted worthy to suffer shame for the Lord Jesus.

When Paul was on the road to Damascus, the voice said, *"Saul, Saul, why persecutest thou me?"* (Acts 9:4). He was persecuting the Lord Jesus' body, the believers. Now Paul is rejoicing that he has the opportunity to suffer for Christ and to fill up the sufferings of Christ. Christ's body is still suffering. There are Christians in prison today, suffering for their faith. Christ feels that. We are His spiritual body.

2. Paul's Ministry of Stewardship

Paul says his ministry is a ministry of stewardship, the stewardship from God which *"is given to me for you"* (v. 25). In Luke 19:11-26 Jesus told the parable about the nobleman who entrusted money to his servants to do business for him while he was away. They were stewards. Paul's stewardship from God was the Word of God, truth from God. He was to be faithful and share it. Jude 3 says defend it; fight for it; don't give it up. Each one of us has been given a stewardship from God. We are stewards of the gift of God. We know salvation. We have the Word of God. We need to be concerned to share it.

3. Paul's Ministry of Salvation

Paul says his ministry is a ministry of salvation. Paul was entrusted with the glorious message of salvation. He was responsible to share this gospel with others. In 1 Corinthians 15:1-4, Paul defines the gospel: Christ died for our sins, He was buried, He rose again the third day and He was seen. This message is the power of God for salvation. If you believe this message, it will result in your salvation. What a glorious message it is! It is not a message of being baptised, joining church or of any works you do. It centers in the Lord Jesus Himself and what He did. There are many people who do not know this message, and they are lost and will die in their sins if they do not hear it. So Paul has a tremendous burden to share this gospel.

Paul speaks of *"the mystery which hath been hid from ages and from generations, but now is made manifest to his saints...which is Christ in you, the hope of glory"* (vv. 26-27). How can Christ be in us? Is He not in heaven? Does Scripture not say *"to wait for his Son from heaven"* (1 Thess. 1:10)? The truth is when you receive the Lord Jesus you also receive the Holy Spirit. All Christians have the Holy Spirit (Rom. 8:9). Paul says the very life of God is in Christians and this life wants to live itself out in us.

4. Paul's Ministry of Sanctification

Paul also says his ministry is a ministry of sanctification. Paul was now concerned for these who had received salvation. He had a warning: beware of sin. Do not fool around with sin. Do not be deceived by sin. Do not jeopardize your usefulness by falling into sin. It is very easy, even if you are saved, to lapse into sin, to do something that would be very destructive in your life and to become useless to the Lord. Paul spoke in 1 Corinthians 9:27 of the fact that he disciplined himself lest, after he had preached to others, he should be disqualified from serving God. There is a battle going on and the devil would like to injure and destroy your life for God.

Paul goes on to say we warn and we teach so that you will grow and develop and go on for the Lord. This was his goal, *"that we may present every man perfect in Christ Jesus"* (v. 28). The idea of *"perfect"* is mature.

When a baby is born, it is a joy! Here is a new person with tremendous potential. The parents have dreams and hopes for their baby. Paul had hopes for his spiritual children, hopes that they would grow up and become mature in Christ Jesus. He was concerned, because not every Christian grows and matures as he should. Paul was not content to see people make a profession. He wanted to see them become mature in the Lord Jesus, to become beautiful Christians. Ephesians 4:12

says, *"For the perfecting of the saints...Till we all come in the unity of the faith...unto a perfect man"* (Eph. 4:12-13).

How do we know if we are growing as Christians? How do we measure our growth? Paul does not say measure yourself by other Christians. No, there is a higher standard than other Christians. Your ultimate goal is the Lord Jesus Himself. He is the One you stand up beside to see how tall you are spiritually. When we do this, we realize that we all have room to grow. We will not reach this standard in this life— *"the measure of the stature of the fulness of Christ"* (Eph. 4:13)—but that is to be our goal, growing in our love for God and becoming like Jesus.

Paul says it is God who is working in me. He was very aware that he could not do the work of God except it be the working of God in him. Paul was *"striving according to his working, which worketh in me mightily"* (v. 29). As Christians we should realize God wants to pour His power through us so that we can do things which, naturally speaking, we could not do. You may say, I don't think I can change; I've got a bad temper and I can never get over it. Paul says, God has been working in me in a wonderful way and He can work mightily in you.

B. Paul's Struggle to See them Grow in their Knowledge of Christ (2:1-5)

For I would that ye knew what great conflict I have for you, and for them at Laodicea, and for as many as have not seen my face in the flesh; That their hearts might be comforted, being knit together in love, and unto all riches of the full assurance of understanding, to the acknowledgement of the mystery of God, and of the Father, and of Christ; In whom are hid all the treasures of wisdom and knowledge. And this I say, lest any man should beguile you with enticing words. For though I be absent in the flesh, yet am I with you in the spirit, joying and beholding your order, and the stedfastness of your faith in Christ.
Colossians 2:1-5

Another goal Paul had was that their hearts would be knit together in love. He longed to see unity and love, harmony and peace among God's children, just as a father longs to see his children getting along with one another.

He speaks also of being intelligent in the things of God. He wants to see them *"attaining to all riches of the full assurance of understanding, to the acknowledgement of the mystery of God"* (v. 2). All the *"treasures of wisdom and knowledge"* (v. 3) are in Christ. He did not want them to be deceived and drawn away from the only source of spiritual understanding.

Paul also desired that they become steadfast, not up and down but steady and strong in their faith. Then he speaks of *"your good order"* (v. 5, NKJV). This is a military concept. It is beautiful to see a military marching unit in step, moving as a group. This is what Paul longed to see among the Christians in Colossae. And Paul says this is my goal for every person, that every one becomes mature in Christ Jesus.

CHAPTER 6

WARNING AGAINST LEGALISM

Colossians 2:6-23

A. Continue in Your Life in Christ (2:6-7)

As ye have therefore received Christ Jesus the Lord,
so walk ye in him: Rooted and built up in him,
and stablished in the faith, as ye have been taught,
abounding therein with thanksgiving.
Colossians 2:6-7

Paul emphasises that Christ is the ultimate of knowledge. The Christians at Colossae wanted to know philosophy and truth. Paul says Christ is the source. In John 14:6 the Lord Jesus said, *"I am the way, the truth, and the life"*. Ephesians 4:21 says *"the truth is in Jesus"*. Do you want to know truth about spiritual matters? The Lord Jesus Christ is the source of truth. You began with the Lord Jesus. Do not go beyond Him. Stay with Him. Become rooted in Him.

B. Beware of False Teachers (2:8)

Beware lest any man spoil you through philosophy
and vain deceit, after the tradition of men, after the
rudiments of the world, and not after Christ.
Colossians 2:8, NKJV

Paul says do not be cheated by getting away from Christ and following other teachings. False religions are off on Christ, either on His Person or His work. False teachers may say Jesus is a good teacher; but they will also say He is not enough, there are other great teachers. Muslims say Jesus is a great teacher—but Mohammed is greater, because he came after Jesus. The Lord Jesus asked His followers, *"Will ye also go away? Then Simon Peter answered him, Lord, to whom shall we go? thou hast the words of eternal life"* (John 6:67-68). The Lord Jesus is uniquely the One with the words of eternal life.

C. Christ is the Fullness of Deity and Authority (2:9-10)

For in him dwelleth all the fulness of the Godhead bodily. And ye are complete in him, which is the head of all principality and power.

Colossians 2:9-10

This is an amazing claim about the Lord Jesus. He is God. Fully God. In His body, God is. In John 8:24 the Lord Jesus said, *"...if ye believe not that I am he, ye shall die in your sins."* You cannot be a Christian if you do not believe that Jesus Christ is God.

As Christians we are complete in the Lord Jesus. We do not need anything else spiritually. The Lord Jesus is enough to save us. He is enough to lead us. He is enough to nourish our spiritual life. He is enough to raise us in the final Day.

D. Spiritual Circumcision of the Flesh, New Life (2:11-12)

In whom also ye are circumcised with the circumcision made without hands, in putting off the body of the sins of the flesh by the circumcision of Christ: Buried with him in baptism, wherein also ye are risen with him through the faith of the operation of God, who hath raised him from the dead.

Colossians 2:11-12

The Christians in Colossae were being bombarded by Jewish teachers who said it was necessary for a Christian to be circumcised and to keep the Jewish Law. Physical circumcision was a literal cutting off part of the flesh and was a sign of the Covenant to a Jewish male. It had come to symbolize the putting off of the evil side of man.

Paul says you were circumcised spiritually in Christ. When you accepted Christ as your Savior you went through a spiritual circumcision of the old life *"putting off the body of the sins of the flesh"* (v. 11) and you became a part of God's people. You do not need to be circumcised physically. Do not go back to the old Law.

You were buried with Christ in baptism. We act out the death, burial and resurrection of the Lord Jesus who was my substitute. We go under the water and come out, picturing our death, burial and resurrection to a new life.

E. The Law Against Us Cancelled (2:13-14)

And you, being dead in your sins and the uncircum-cision of your flesh, hath he quickened together with him, having forgiven you all trespasses; Blotting out the handwriting of ordinances that was against us, which was contrary to us, and took it out of the way, nailing it to his cross. Colossians 2:13-14

Every one of us has broken the Ten Commandments, God's Law. Broken laws have a penalty and the law becomes our adversary. In Galatians 3:13 Paul says, *"Christ hath redeemed us from the curse of the law, being made a curse for us: for it is written, Cursed is every one that hangeth on a tree"*. The debt of our sins was nailed to the Lord Jesus' cross. He paid the penalty in full. His death satisfies the Law. All our sins have been forgiven and we have been made alive in Christ.

F. Evil Angelic Forces Defeated by the Cross (2:15)

Having disarmed principalities and powers, He made a public spectacle of them, triumphing over them in it. Colossians 2:15, NKJV

Paul here describes the tremendous victory the Lord Jesus won. All the forces of evil were defeated at the cross. This is potentially true and will be realized in a coming day when He sets up His kingdom. Paul pictures this glorious victory, as he no doubt has heard of and seen Roman triumphant marches. At the head of this parade he sees the cross as carried high, a symbol of that victory.

G. Reject Jewish Legalism, Festivals and Mysticism (2:16-19)

Let no man therefore judge you in meat, or in drink, or in respect of an holyday, or of the new moon, or of the sabbath days: Which are a shadow of things to come; but the body is of Christ. Let no man beguile you of your reward in a voluntary humility and worshipping of angels, intruding into those things which he hath not seen, vainly puffed up by his fleshly mind, And not holding the Head, from which all the body by joints and bands having nourishment ministered, and knit together, increaseth with the increase of God.

Colossians 2:16-19

The sacrifices and rituals of the Old Testament could not take away sin. They were a shadow of what was to come. Behind them was the reality of Christ Himself. Paul says do not go back to the shadows. Christ has come! For a Gentile the danger is not of going back to Judaism but of keeping church rules, rules added on to receiving Christ for salvation, such as baptism.

Paul also warns against spiritism. Christ has defeated Satan's forces. Do not worship angels; do not contact the spirit world; stay away from witchcraft. These areas are dangerous and useless for Christian growth. Instead, hold fast to the Head. Spiritual nourishment for a Christian comes from our head, the Lord Jesus. Focus on Christ.

H. You Died with Christ; Do Not Go Back to Food Laws or Asceticism (2:20-23)

Wherefore if ye be dead with Christ from the rudiments of the world, why, as though living in the world, are ye subject to ordinances, (Touch not; taste not; handle not; Which all are to perish with the using;) after the commandments and doctrines of men? Which things have indeed a shew of wisdom in will worship, and humility, and neglecting of the body; not in any honour to the satisfying of the flesh. Colossians 2:20-23

As believers we do many things to please the Lord but not to gain salvation. Man's religion is based on what you do to get right with God. Paul says reject legalism. Rules have no value against the flesh. They will not make you holy. Focus on the Lord Jesus Christ to give you the power to change.

CHAPTER 7

HOLY LIVING
PART ONE

Colossians 3:1-9a

As was his custom, Paul begins the book of Colossians with a doctrinal basis of the Christian life. He then goes on to build on this foundation with his practical exhortations.

A. Motivation: Focus on Christ and Heaven (3:1-4)

> *If ye then be risen with Christ, seek those things which are above, where Christ sitteth on the right hand of God. Set your affection on things above, not on things on the earth. For ye are dead, and your life is hid with Christ in God. When Christ, who is our life, shall appear, then shall ye also appear with him in glory.* Colossians 3:1-4

In this passage Paul goes back to this doctrinal statement he made regarding Christians. He states that we were raised with Christ and seated with Him in heavenly places. He thus emphasizes our position in God's sight. We are already in heaven itself, seated with Christ. Our life is wrapped up with Christ. In view of this, our lives on earth should reveal our new position. So he says, *"Set your affection on things above, not on things on the earth"* (v. 2). Feed yourself from the Word of God. Fellowship with other Christians. Focus on Christ and your life in Him.

Paul looks forward to the time when Christ is coming back and he states that, when He appears, we *"shall also appear with him in glory"* (v. 4). And he now gets into some very practical areas. Paul was a great theologian but he never stopped there. He got down to earth itself, where the believers were living.

B. Put to Death your Sinful Nature: Sexual Sins, Evil Desires, Greed, Rage, Slander, Filthy Talk, Lying (3:5-9)

> *Mortify therefore your members which are upon the earth; fornication, uncleanness, inordinate affection, evil concupiscence, and covetousness, which is idolatry: For which things' sake the wrath of God cometh on the children of disobedience: In the which ye also walked some time, when ye lived in them. But now ye also put off all these; anger, wrath, malice, blasphemy, filthy communication out of your mouth. Lie not one to another, seeing that ye have put off the old man with his deeds;*
>
> Colossians 3:5-9

From the beginning Paul makes it clear that there is a negative side to Christianity, a putting to death of the life that we once lived. He emphasizes that our speech should reveal our new life. There are things that are to be omitted from our lives, things which once characterized our lives as unbelievers.

Paul begins by mentioning fornication, a term which applies to all sexual sins. The Commandment is *"Thou shalt not commit adultery"* (Ex. 20:14). But in Leviticus 18 God amplifies this to show what He regards as being adultery. It is not just the narrow way we tend to use the word. Leviticus 18 details the many forms of sexual sin that God hates. It, of course, includes adultery as we think of it as it applies to a married man who is unfaithful to his wife. It goes on to include all forms of sexual activity outside of marriage: sex between unmarried people, homosexuality and bestiality. God in creation gives instructions in Genesis 1. He created sex for the purpose of procreation. It is a very fierce drive, dominant in all species, and its goal is the passing on of life. So he says *"Be fruitful and multiply"* (Gen. 1:28).

The Lord Jesus said in Matthew 5:27-28, *"Ye have heard that it was said by them of old time, Thou shalt not commit adultery: But I say unto you, That whosoever looketh on a woman to lust after her hath committed adultery with her already in his heart."* Sexual fantasies are sin and lead to sinful actions. It matters what you see and think. If you want to be holy and live a life for God, you must control this area.

Today there is a tremendous surge of interest in homosexuality. It is affirmed that it is a natural drive that some people have. In other words, people are born as homosexual and to restrict their activity in any form is to deny what God has created. And so we see laws being passed legalizing homosexual activity. But God condemns homosexuality in both the Old and the New Testament. It is strongly condemned in Leviticus 18. In Romans 1 it is seen as being the depth of sexual perversion. In 1 Corinthians 6:9-10, Scripture affirms that this activity is hated by God. So we may say that all sexual sin is potentially in the heart of man, but God says that homosexual sin is a perversion of what He has created.

The Scripture goes on to describe sin as that which produces uncleanness. The sinner, when he confronts the holiness of God, has a tremendous sense of filth and dirt. When he comes to know salvation, there is a release from this and it is pictured by baptism, the washing away of the old life.

The word passion emphasizes the intensity of feeling which must be reserved for the marriage relationship. Passion and evil desire are coupled together in this passage and he stresses that these are to be put aside.

Covetousness, of course, is greed. It manifests itself in various forms, but ordinarily we think of this as connected with money. Paul calls covetousness idolatry. In 1 Timothy 6:6-10 he warns against the love of money which is *"the root of all evil: which while some coveted after, they have erred from the faith, and pierced themselves through with many sorrows"* (v. 10). Instead he says be content with food and clothing.

The Scripture emphasizes that God hates sin. He is angry with the sinner. And the Christian who sets his mind on things above will come to hate that which God hates also. We once lived that way and our thinking was completely twisted and perverted by sin. Now we have God's perspective on sin. So Paul says you once lived in them—not any more.

Paul describes the old ways of living as filthy garments to be put off. He continues with anger, wrath, malice, blasphemy and filthy language. The first three are sins that are sometimes accepted by Christians. It is easy to justify anger, wrath and malice when we claim to be righteously angry. And sin should make us angry. But the Scripture says, *"Be ye angry, and sin not"* (Eph. 4:26) and *"the wrath of man worketh not the righteousness of God"* (Jas. 1:20). There is much coarse speaking today. Filthy language is to be expunged from one's vocabulary. Put off these filthy garments.

Lying is to be avoided. The Christian is to tell the truth. The Lord Jesus Himself said, *"I am...the truth"* (John 14:6). Christians need to be deeply concerned about this matter. It is easy to tell half-truths, to tell that which is not transparent and true. Society is filled with prevarications. The Christian is to be different from the world. The Christian must resolve to be truthful.

The commandment *"Lie not one to another"* (v. 9), is absolute. And yet there are times when the believer is in a difficult position. One thinks of Rahab the harlot with a choice, either to tell the truth and to see the men executed, or to lie and to spare their lives. In a situation like this, the believer must choose the lesser of two evils. Scripture gives examples of David and others who lied in order to save their own lives or the lives of others. And the Scriptures indicate they did the right thing.

> Have Thine own way, Lord!
> Have Thine own way!
> Thou art the Potter; I am the clay
> Mould me and make me

After Thy will,
While I am waiting,
Yielded and still.

Have Thine own way, Lord!
Have Thine own way!
Hold o'er my being
Absolute sway!
Fill with Thy Spirit
Till all shall see
Christ only, always,
Living in me!

Adelaide A. Pollard,
November 27, 1862 - December 20, 1934

CHAPTER 8

HOLY LIVING
PART TWO

Colossians 3:9b-17

A. You Have Put on the New Man,
Which Needs Daily Renewal (3:9b-11)

...seeing that ye have put off the old man with his deeds; And have put on the new man, which is renewed in knowledge after the image of him that created him: Where there is neither Greek nor Jew, circumcision nor uncircumcision, Barbarian, Scythian, bond nor free: but Christ is all, and in all.
Colossians 3:9b-11

The Christian life is to be different. Paul speaks of the new way of living as new clothes which one puts on. These are to be put on daily. You put off the old way of life. You are now to put on the new. This takes place initially at conversion but then it is to be renewed daily. It is not a once for all procedure. It would be nice if we could say we have put off the old man for good. But old habits have a way of hanging on and one discovers that, even though he is born again, his old ways of thinking and doing reoccur again and again. So this is an exhortation for believers whether they are young believers or old.

The model that the Christian is to follow is that of the Lord Jesus, and as we think of Him in all His perfection we will all realize our own lack. He is the head of the body, the church. This church is composed of both Jew and Gentile and barbarian (that is, non-Greek speaking or uneducated.) It includes all who put their trust in the Lord Jesus.

B. Clothe Yourself Daily with Compassion, Kindness, Humility, Gentleness, Patience, Forgiveness and Love Over All (3:12-14)

Put on therefore, as the elect of God, holy and beloved, bowels of mercies, kindness, humbleness of mind, meekness, longsuffering; Forbearing one another, and forgiving one another, if any man have a quarrel against any: even as Christ forgave you, so also do ye. And above all these things put on charity, which is the bond of perfectness.

Colossians 3:12-14

The believer is to be marked by these Christian virtues. The first that is mentioned is mercy, to have a heart that is moved by the suffering around us. Next is kindness, which is an action of compassion to meet the needs of the person in need. One thinks of the example of the Good Samaritan. The Lord Jesus tells of him going along that road down to Jericho. He sees a man who has been set upon by outlaws and lies there wounded and dying. He not only feels compassion for him, but that compassion moves him to meet his needs. So he binds up his wounds, sets him on his donkey and takes him down to the inn where he is to spend the night. One can see the compassion that moved him to this act of kindness.

The Christian life is to be a life of humility. He is constantly aware of his own weakness. He has no right to feel any pride. His life as a follower of the Lord Jesus is to be marked by forgiveness. He has been forgiven so much himself that he cannot afford to be unforgiving toward others. When asked by Peter how many times to forgive, the Lord Jesus said, *"seventy times seven"* (Matt. 18:22). There is never a time when one can say I refuse to forgive any more.

The great and second commandment, which the Lord Jesus said sums up all other commandments, is to love one another. This is not love as we often think of it today. It is not simply affection based on emotion. It is a determined spirit of forgiveness and acceptance of that person, a decision to do him good. It is an act of the will, a decision to do well for that person through life. When we think of the Christian life, we think of love as that outer garment that covers it all. If we love one another, we will fulfill the Law of Christ.

C. Aids to Godliness: a Heart at Peace Filled with God's Word, Sharing the Word and Singing, Doing all in Christ's Name (3:15-17)

And let the peace of God rule in your hearts, to the which also ye are called in one body; and be ye thankful. Let the word of Christ dwell in you richly in all wisdom; teaching and admonishing one another in psalms and hymns and spiritual songs, singing with grace in your hearts to the Lord. And whatsoever ye do in word or deed, do all in the name of the Lord Jesus, giving thanks to God and the Father by him.

Colossians 3:15-17

The believer is to always have the peace of God in his heart, a sense of confidence, knowing he is doing the will of God. Any sin coming in will disturb that tranquility of spirit which God desires us to have. This *"peace of God"* (v. 15) will be manifest in the body of Christ as we meet with the Lord's people and it is manifest in singing and rejoicing together. Singing is something that has characterized God's people through the years. In singing we unite to praise the Lord and to worship Him. In singing we unite to exhort one another to persevere in the faith. Singing is a means of edifying the body of Christ. It has always been that which has accompanied real spiritual life.

The Lord's people are exhorted to do everything in life in the name of the Lord Jesus. This will sanctify life and make it meaningful. In the morning when one awakens he can commit the day to the Lord, and in all the decisions of life he can pray for the Lord's guidance and leading. If there is any unease or distress of spirit he should take warning. This will guard him from making any foolish and costly errors. And constantly, as he goes through life, he is to cultivate a thankful spirit. How good God has been to him!

> In the shadow of Thy wings
>> I will sing for joy;
> What a God, who out of shade
>> Nest for singing bird hath made!
> Lord, my Might and Melody,
>> I will sing to Thee.
>
> If the shadow of Thy wings
>> Be so full of song,
> What must be the lighted place
>> Where Thy bird can see Thy face?
> Lord, my Might and Melody,
>> I will sing to Thee.
>
> Amy Carmichael,
> December 16, 1867 - January 18, 1951

CHAPTER 9

HOLY FAMILIES

Colossians 3:18-4:6

A. Wives to Submit to Husbands (3:18)

Wives, submit yourselves unto your own husbands,
as it is fit in the Lord.   Colossians 3:18

Paul in several passages of Scripture gives instruction to the family. The exhortation he gives to wives is to submit, to submit to their husbands. This was the first commandment given to the wife in Genesis 3 and it is a very important Scripture today. The human heart is a heart of a rebel. The natural tendency is to want to throw off any restraint. It is especially hard for a wife to be submissive to her husband in this day in which we live. And yet the wife here is exhorted to be submissive, not to be a rebel.

B. Husbands to Love Wives (3:19)

Husbands, love your wives, and be not bitter against
them.   Colossians 3:19

The word to the husband is to love your wife. This is not just simply affection but it is a deep concern for the well being and happiness of the wife. Satan would do all he can to disrupt the affection you should feel for your wife. There is always another woman to excite the interest of a man. Here he must be resolute and determined to love his wife. And if he has love for her, she will find it easier to submit. The man is also encouraged not to be bitter against his wife. He should be a model of forgiveness toward her. Over the course of time there are bound to be some differences of opinion. Here the wife must learn ultimately to submit to the husband's wishes and he in turn must be endlessly forgiving towards her, because the truth is, in many points we all stumble.

C. Children to Obey Parents; Fathers to be Gentle (3:20-21)

Children, obey your parents in all things: for this is well pleasing unto the Lord. Fathers, provoke not your children to anger, lest they be discouraged.
Colossians 3:20-21

Children are exhorted to obey their parents. We live in a world where young people do not show respect for elders and where a Christian family must maintain godly order. In a world of disobedience a godly home is a powerful testimony to the work of God. The world needs to have such models to emulate.

Fathers are given a word of exhortation here with regard to their children. Do not be too harsh and demanding. Children should know the rules of the family and should abide by them. And fathers should not be too demanding and expect too much of them. And constantly the children should realize their father does love them and there is forgiveness in the family.

D. Slaves, Servants, be Obedient; Work for the Lord (3:22-25)

Servants, obey in all things your masters according to the flesh; not with eyeservice, as menpleasers; but in singleness of heart, fearing God: And whatsoever ye do, do it heartily, as to the Lord, and not unto men; Knowing that of the Lord ye shall receive the reward of the inheritance: for ye serve the Lord Christ. But he that doeth wrong shall receive for the wrong which he hath done: and there is no respect of persons.
Colossians 3:22-25

Paul shifts to give some instruction concerning slaves. Many families owned slaves. It was a common institution in the Roman Empire. His word of exhortation is to obey, realizing that by obeying you are pleasing God. Do what you do for your master whole-heartedly, as to God Himself. Paul does not tell them to have a spirit of rebellion. This is all too common even today. Instead he says, you be submissive and do what you do for the Lord. There are principles that carry over even today as we think of workers and their employers. Be submissive and be whole-hearted and do what you do for the Lord. If you do this, you will be acknowledged in today's workplace. Your faithfulness will be appreciated.

E. Masters, be Fair and Kind (4:1)

Masters, give unto your servants that which is just and equal; knowing that ye also have a Master in heaven. Colossians 4:1

Paul addresses masters, which would include both those who are over slaves they own and those who are over servants they do not own. The commandment is to employers. Treat your employees the way you would like to be treated. Be fair and honest. You have a master in heaven who will one day require an accounting. In the previous verse, workers have been encouraged to work heartily as to the Lord. The day is coming when there will be a general accounting both how we have served the Lord and, as employers, how we have treated our employees.

F. Further Advice (4:2-6)

The section begins with a variety of instructions. One could call it "Instructions for the Church." The church often met in homes, as is mentioned in the verses that follow. It was like a family, and as such it was marked by intimacy and familiarity in dealing with one another. The church is not primarily a building but an assembly, a congregation. The building houses the church. So we think of this as being family talk within the church.

We see Paul naming many people. It is a source of constant amazement how many people he knew intimately. One must remember that the Roman Empire was a great unifying force in those days. You could cross from one country to another and there were no tolls or passport regulations to conform to. There was a marvellous system of roads throughout the Roman Empire so that it made travel very easy. This explains why Paul had so many contacts scattered abroad.

1. Pray Much, Especially for Paul (4:2-4)

> *Continue in prayer, and watch in the same with thanksgiving; Withal praying also for us, that God would open unto us a door of utterance, to speak the mystery of Christ, for which I am also in bonds: That I may make it manifest, as I ought to speak.*
> Colossians 4:2-4

Paul requests prayer for himself that he may have wisdom in presenting the gospel. Wherever he was he wanted to be a good servant of Jesus Christ. He was determined to be a good witness regardless of his circumstances.

Now we do not want to visualize Paul as being in prison as we know it today. He was under what we would call house arrest. The last of Acts pictures him in this way. Although he was chained to a Roman soldier, he could receive his friends and he could write letters. He had a great degree of liberty while he was waiting trial, and Paul wants them to pray for real liberty in preaching the gospel. Whether in prison or free he wants to be a good witness to the grace of God. He was constantly driven by the realization he was surrounded by people who needed this message.

2. Be Wise in Your Witnessing (4:5-6)

> *Walk in wisdom toward them that are without, redeeming the time. Let your speech be always*

with grace, seasoned with salt, that ye may know
how ye ought to answer every man.

Colossians 4:5-6

He wants them to be good witnesses, being wise in their witness to others. Wherever a person is, there are some who need to hear the gospel, whether you are in bonds or free. Paul realizes too that your speech must be with grace, constantly being aware that the person to whom you are witnessing is precious and is very, very lost.

CHAPTER 10

CONCLUDING GREETINGS

Colossians 4:7-18

A. Tychicus and Onesimus Will Give the News About Me (4:7-9)

Tychicus, a beloved brother, faithful minister, and fellow servant in the Lord, will tell you all the news about me. I am sending him to you for this very purpose, that he may know your circumstances and comfort your hearts, with Onesimus, a faithful and beloved brother, who is one of you. They will make known to you all things which are happening here.
Colossians 4:7-9, NKJV

Tychicus is being sent with a message from Paul to bring them up to date on his present circumstances. He was a faithful man, a good man, and he comes to them now with news concerning Paul. Paul also includes Onesimus, a slave who was converted during his contacts with Paul. Paul writes concerning him in the book to Philemon, his owner, and he pleads for lenience in connection with Onesimus, his child in the faith. He is sending him back now to set things right with his master.

This gives us insight into the problem that confronted the people of that day. If one was a slave before conversion, he was one after conversion. But now there was a new relationship between master and slave. He was a brother in the Lord. In some cases the master would no doubt let the slave go free. But Paul does not require this of the owner. It may seem difficult for us to realize that perhaps in every church there were a number of slaves. Some had masters who had been converted. Some did not. In either case, they were called upon to be a good slave and to be wholehearted in their work.

B. Aristarchus, a Fellow Prisoner, Mark, Justus, who are Jews, Send Greetings (4:10-11)

> *Aristarchus my fellowprisoner saluteth you, and Marcus, sister's son to Barnabas, (touching whom ye received commandments: if he come unto you, receive him;) And Jesus, which is called Justus, who are of the circumcision. These only are my fellow-workers unto the kingdom of God, which have been a comfort unto me.* Colossians 4:10-11

Paul also mentions a few others. Aristarchus is named and then Mark is mentioned. He had disappointed Paul on their first missionary journey, turning back rather than going on with them. In fact Paul and Barnabas quit working together over that issue. Mark had turned back from the work and Paul felt he was not ready to go on in the service of the Lord. But this is years later and Mark has proved himself and now he has Paul's commendation. Paul was not one to hold grudges. He had a big heart for God and His people. We know nothing further about the Jesus mentioned here. Jesus was a common name among the Jews. But these were some of God's children whom Paul mentions, commending them.

C. Epaphras, One of You, Prays Much for You, Laodicea and Hierapolis (4:12-13)

> *Epaphras, who is one of you, a bondservant of Christ, greets you, always laboring fervently for you in prayers, that you may stand perfect and complete in all the will of God. For I bear him witness that he has a great zeal for you, and those who are in Laodicea, and those in Hierapolis.*
> Colossians 4:12-13

Epaphras receives Paul's highest commendation. He has a great heart for the saints in Colosse and for the Lord's work in general. Even though he is not with them at present they are in his heart.

D. Dr. Luke and Demas Send Greetings (4:14)

Luke the beloved physician and Demas greet you.
Colossians 4:14

He goes on to speak of Luke. He describes him as the beloved physician, a doctor. Luke has been a part of Paul's party since he joined them prior to the first visit to Philippi. Paul may have felt the need for doctoring at certain times. We do not know his ailments but we know that he had certain disfiguring problems at times. There is no point in speculating as to the nature of his problems. His request was that the Lord remove his thorn in the flesh but the Lord said His grace was sufficient (2 Cor. 12:9).

Demas is also mentioned. At this time he was apparently still working with Paul, a part of his team. It is sad that as Paul comes to the end of life he speaks of Demas as having forsaken him (2 Tim. 4:10). It is sad when you realize that one may serve God and later in life turn away. It is a warning to us all.

E. Greet Brothers in Laodicea and the Church in Nympha's House (4:15)

Give my greetings to the brothers and sisters at Laodicea, and to Nympha and the church in her house.
Colossians 4:15, NIV

Paul mentions here the church in Nympha's house and also the church in Laodicia, and he sends his warm greetings to them. Most of the churches in that day were in homes. 1 Corinthians 14:26 speaks of the informality and participation in those churches, "...*when ye come together, every one of you hath a psalm, hath a doctrine, hath a tongue, hath a revelation, hath an interpretation. Let all things be done unto edifying."* They were a family of God, sharing the Word of God.

F. Share Letters with Laodicea (4:16)

And when this epistle is read among you, cause that it be read also in the church of the Laodiceans; and that ye likewise read the epistle from Laodicea.
Colossians 4:16

He speaks of the churches and urges them to share his writings. These were letters to be shared with one another as members of the body of Christ. We do not have any epistle today to Laodicia. Apparently it was not considered inspired and was not included in the Canon of God's Word. All of Paul's writings, apparently, were not considered inspired.

G. Archipus, Finish Your Work (4:17)

And say to Archippus, Take heed to the ministry which thou hast received in the Lord, that thou ful-fil it.
Colossians 4:17

He then writes a word of exhortation to Archipus who had received a ministry from God, and now Paul exhorts him to carry out the ministry. It is a word of exhortation for all of God's people today.

H. Remember My Chains. Grace Be with You. Hand Written, Paul (4:18)

The salutation by the hand of me Paul. Remember my bonds. Grace be with you. Amen.
Colossians 4:18, NKJV

Paul apparently did not write all his letters. He often used amanuenses, and in this case, he pens his own signature. He wants them to realize this really is a letter from him. He reminds his readers of his bonds. Paul often backs up his writings by a reminder of his sufferings for them. All his sufferings are the evidence of his reality.

Then he closes the letter, *"Grace be with you."* It is a favorite closing of his, his invocation of grace upon them. Paul delighted in the grace of God. And his parting to them is grace.

It is a fitting way to conclude this letter.

> O to grace how great a debtor
> Daily I'm constrained to be!
> Let that grace, Lord, like a fetter,
> Bind my wand'ring heart to Thee.
> Robert Robinson,
September 27, 1735 - June 9.1790

BIBLIOGRAPHY

Alford, Henry, *The Greek Testament*, Vols. I-III (Boston: Lee and Shepherd, 1874).

Bauer, Walter, *A Greek-English Lexicon of the New Testament, trans.* by William F. Arndt and F. Wilbur Gingrich, fourth edition (Chicago: University of Chicago, 1957).

Bruce, F.F., *The Acts of the Apostles*, Greek Text (London: Tyndale Press, 1951).

Commentary on the Book of the Acts, English Text (Grand Rapids: Wm. B. Eerdmans, 1954).

Jesus: Lord & Savior (Downers Grove: InterVarsity Press,1986).

Paul: Apostle of the Heart Set Free (Grand Rapids: Wm. B.Eerdmans, 1977).

Peter, Stephen, James, and John (Grand Rapids: Wm. B. Eerdmans, 1979).

Bible Commentary (Grand Rapids: Zondervan, 1986)

Conybeare, W.J. and Howson, J.S., *The Life and the Epistles of St. Paul* (Grand Rapids: Wm. B. Eerdmans, 1950).

Dictionary of the Apostolic Church, edited by James Hastings (Edinburgh: T & T Clark, 1915).

Dictionary of Christ and the Gospels, edited by James Hastings (Edinburgh: T & T Clark, 1906).

Dictionary of Jesus and the Gospels, edited by Joel B. Green and Scot McKnight (Downers Grove: InterVarsity Press, 1992).

Dictionary of Paul and His Letters, edited by Gerald F. Hawthorne, Ralph P. Martin, Daniel G. Reid. (Downers Grove: InterVarsity Press, 1994)

Edersheim, Alfred, *The Life and Times of Jesus the Messiah*, two volumes (Grand Rapids: Wm.B. Eerdmans, 1947).

Sketches of Jewish Social Life in the Days of Christ (London: The Religious Tract Society, undated).

The Temple and Its Services (London: The Religious Tract Society, undated).

Ellicott, Charles J., *Commentary on the Whole Bible* (Grand Rapids: Zondervan, 1959).

Commentary on Philippians, Colossians, and Philemon (Andover:Warren F. Draper, 1872)

Expositor's Greek Testament (Grand Rapids: Wm. B. Eerdmans, 1970).

Geldenhuys, Norval, *Commentary on the Gospel of Luke* (Grand Rapids: Wm. B. Eerdmans, 1951).

Godet, F., *The Gospel of Luke* (Edinburgh: T. & T. Clark, 1870).

Harnack, Adolph, *Luke, the Physician* (New York: Putnam's Sons, 1911).

Hort, F.J.A., *The Christian Ecclesia* (London: MacMillan and Co.,1900).

International Bible Encyclopaedia, edited by Geoffrey W. Bromiley (Grand Rapids: Wm. B. Eerdmans, 1979).

Josephus, Flavius, *Josephus: Complete Works*, trans. by William Whiston (Grand

Rapids: Kregel, 1963)

Knowling, R.J., *The Acts of the Apostles in The Expositor's Greek Testament* (Grand Rapids: Wm. B. Eerdmans, 1970).

Latourette, Kenneth Scott, *A History of Christianity* (New York: Harper & Row, 1953).

Lenski, R. C. H., *An Interpretation of St. Paul's Epistles to the Galatians, Ephesians and Philippians* (Columbus, Ohio: The Wartbur Press, 1946).

Lindsay, T. M., *The Church and the Ministry in the Early Centuries* (London: Hodder and Stoughton, 1903).

MacDonald, William, *Believers Bible Commentary* (Wichita:

A & O Press, 1989).

McGifffert, Arthur C., *A History of Christianity in the Apostolic Age* (Edinburgh: T & T Clark, 1897).

Meyer, Heinrich A. W., *The Acts of the Apostles* (New York: Funk & Wagnalls, 1889).

Meyer, Heinrich A.W., *The Gospels of Mark and Luke* (New York: Funk & Wagnalls, 1889).

Marshall, I. Howard, *The Gospel of Luke* (Greek text) (Grand Rapids: Wm.B. Eerdmans, 1978).

Moulton, James Hope and George Milligan, *Vocabulary of the Greek Testament* (London: Hodder and Stoughton, 1949).

Moulton, W.F. and A. S. Geden, *A Concordance to the Greek Testament* (Edinburgh: T & T Clark, 1906).

New Bible Dictionary edited by J. D. Douglas (Grand Rapids: Wm. B. Eerdmans, 1962).

Ramsay, William M., *Historical Geography of Asia Minor* (London: John Murray, 1890).

A Historical Commentary on St. Paul's Epistle to the Galatians (London: Hodder and Stoughton, 1899).

St. Paul the Traveler and Roman Citizen (London: Hodder and Stoughton, 1898).

The Church in the Roman Empire (London: Hodder and Stoughton, 1900).

Samarin, William J., *Tongues of Men and Angels* (New York: Macmillan, 1972).

Schaff, Philip, *History of the Christian Church* (Grand Rapids: Wm. B. Eerdmans, 1970).

Stott, John, *The Spirit, the Church and the World* (Downers Grove: InterVarsity Press, 1990).

Theological Dictionary of the New Testament edited by G. Kittel and G. Friedrich, trans. by Geoffrey W. Bromiley (Grand Rapids: Wm. B. Eerdmans, 1964).

OTHER BOOKS BY DONALD NORBIE

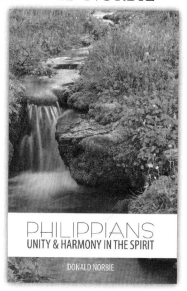

Galatians: Liberty in Christ

In the book of Galatians the apostle Paul is determined to defend the gospel of grace.

Paul had once been the most legalistic of Jews. In Christ, God revealed to him that one is saved by grace through faith without works. This is a message that needs to be trumpeted in every age and never more than today.

Galatians: Liberty in Christ seeks to unpack the epistle for the believer, drawing on the author's knowledge of the Greek text. May it affirm for God's people the awesome truth that one is saved by grace alone through faith alone.

Philippians: Unity & Harmony in the Spirit

Take time to go through the book of Philippians, with this book as a companion, and glean truths from God's Word to learn more about Him.

How did Paul serve the Lord? Paul constantly referred to himself as an example for believers to follow (1 Cor. 11:1). He was aware that he was the Lord's slave, accountable to Him (Gal. 1:10). This caused him to speak God's Word without the fear of men. Paul and the early apostles and preachers served the Lord in faith, trusting Him daily for their needs. They looked to the Lord for direction in their service for Him.

OTHER BOOKS BY DONALD NORBIE

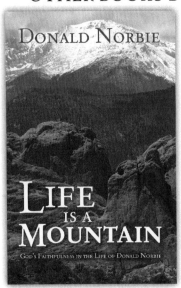

Life is a Mountain: God's Faithfulness in the Life of Donald Norbie

This biography is written that it may be a blessing to others. It is my desire to glorify the Lord, to show how He saved a teenage boy and faithfully preserved him through all the experiences of life. God is faithful! My prayer is that the reading of this account may be used by God to draw some to the Saviour in salvation and to encourage them to pursue discipleship of the Lord Jesus. There is no better life and it brings eternal reward. *"For bodily exercise profits a little, but godliness is profitable for all things, having promise of the life that now is and of that which is to come"* (1 Tim. 4:8).

Mountains & Valleys in Christian Living

This book covers several important subjects. These topics have been selected by the author as he reflects on his own personal Christian life with it's challenges, trials, and triumphs, work and witness, study and sharing during the different stages of his life.

These truths are shared with the readers to encourage them to always put the Lord first in their lives. It will not always be easy but we should be motivated to serve the Lord who purchased us with His own precious blood. He reminds us that our life of service is the only reasonable thing we can give our Master.

OTHER BOOKS BY DONALD NORBIE

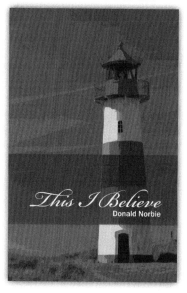

The Parables: Truth Illuminated

The parables were a powerful teaching tool that our Lord used often. Doctrine presented in abstract terms may seem dry and cold. The parables make doctrine come alive, flesh it out, make it vibrant and pulsating with life. They fasten themselves upon one's memory and are embedded in our heritage. Parables such as The Good Samaritan and The Prodigal Son are often quoted in literature. It is hoped that this book will help the reader understand and better appreciate the message our Lord wished to give.

This I Believe

This book by Donald Norbie will outline some of the principles and doctrines he has observed in the careful study of God's Word.

It is important for Christians to spend valuable time in the personal study of God's Word. The instructions needed for daily living, church life, worship, witness and service will be found therein. As you read through this book you will have the opportunity to be instructed and guided by a man that started searching the Scriptures as a teenager, and devoted much of his time to personal study and the teaching of believers following their personal acceptance of the Lord Jesus as Saviour.

BOOKLETS BY DONALD NORBIE

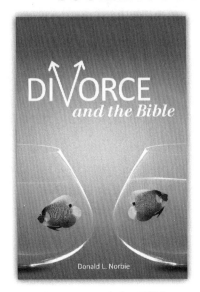

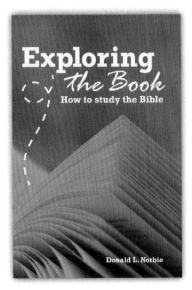

Divorce and the Bible

In the midst of the seething currents of modern, permissive thought, the Word of God stand like a rock. God's eternal principles don't change and are for man's good (Deut. 6:24). True happiness is still to be found when one woman and one man take their marriage vows seriously and live together in love and faithfulness until death parts them.

And yet the Lord is able to heal the ravages of sin. It is the prayer of the author that this book will lead Christians to a better understanding of this problem that devastates so many lives.

Exploring the Book: How to Study the Bible

Paul, in his last two letters to Timothy, emphasizes the importance of the Word of God, the Bible. *"All scripture is given by inspiration of God and is profitable for doctrine, for reproof, for correction, for instruction in righteousness"* (2 Tim. 3:16). This is a tremendous claim for any book. Other books may be helpful tools but one must remember that it is the Bible itself that is the channel for spiritual life from God.